Funniest Minibeasts

by Annabelle Lynch

W
FRANKLIN WATTS
LONDON·SYDNEY

First published in 2012 by
Franklin Watts
338 Euston Road
London
NW1 3BH

Franklin Watts Australia
Level 17/207 Kent Street
Sydney
NSW 2000

Copyright © Franklin Watts 2012

Picture credits:
Shutterstock: front cover, 4cr, 5b, 7, 8, 11, 18. 20.
David Cappaert/MSU/Bugwood.org: 5t, 12.
istockphoto: 4cl, 15, 16.

Every attempt has been made to clear copyright.
Should there be any inadvertent omission please
apply to the publisher for rectification.

A CIP catalogue record for this book is
available from the British Library.

Dewey number: 592

ISBN 978 1 4451 0324 2 (hbk)
ISBN 978 1 4451 0332 7 (pbk)

Series Editor: Melanie Palmer
Picture Researcher: Diana Morris
Series Advisor: Catherine Glavina
Series Designer: Peter Scoulding

Printed in China

Franklin Watts is a division of Hachette Children's Books,
an Hachette UK company. www.hachette.co.uk

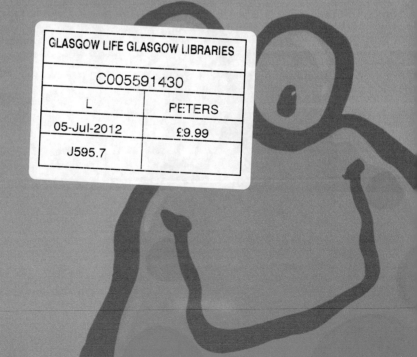

Contents

The words in **bold** can be found in the glossary.

What is a minibeast?

A minibeast is a tiny animal. There are many kinds, from slimy snails to buzzing **insects**.

 Creepy crawlies

Minibeasts do not have a **backbone**. Their bodies are often protected by a hard outer case.

There are no bones inside a minibeast.

What do minibeasts eat?

Some minibeasts eat plants. Some eat animals. Beetles and spiders **hunt**, and eat other animals.

Spiders trap their prey in a sticky web, then eat them later.

Home habitats

Minibeasts can live anywhere! Spot them in your home, on the beach, in the soil or in the trees.

Caterpillars crawl on leaves and eat them all day long!

Defence or attack!

12

Earwigs have pincers that can give you a nasty nip!

Many minibeasts look scary,
but most won't hurt you.
Some can give a bite or sting.

Minibeast moves

Minibeasts can fly, crawl, slide, run and jump. Some have lots of legs so they can run away fast!

The name centipede means 100 feet but really they have much fewer!

Slimy trails

Slugs and snails leave a slimy, sticky trail wherever they go. Look out for them in gardens.

Snails also use slime to slide in and out of their shells.

Strong minibeasts

Some minibeasts are very strong. Ants can carry a lot more than their own body weight!

Ants have the biggest brains of all insects!

Busy minibeasts

Minibeasts help in the natural cycle. Bees collect **nectar** from flowers, to help flowers make their **seeds**.

Bees use nectar from flowers to make honey.

Glossary

Backbone – a line of bone along the back

Hunt – find and kill animals for food

Insect – type of animal that has six legs and a body in three parts

Nectar – sticky sweet liquid in a flower

Seed – new plants grow from a seed

Websites:

http://www.mylearning.org/minibeasts/p-468/
http://www.pestworldforkids.org/ants.html
http://www.bbc.co.uk/schools/teachers/breathing-places/class_activities/minibeast_corner.shtml

Quiz

1.   Which minibeast eats all day long?

2.   What do bees do?

3.   Which minibeast is very strong?

4.   Which minibeast has many legs?

5.   How can you follow a snail?

6.   Which minibeast spins a web?

The answers are on page 24

1. The caterpillar
2. Make honey from nectar in flowers
3. The ant
4. The centipede
5. By its slimy trail
6. The spider

Index